LEBRON JAMES

BY RYAN NAGELHOUT

Gareth Stevens
PUBLISHING

Please visit our website, www.garethstevens.com. For a free color catalog of all our high-quality books, call toll free 1-800-542-2595 or fax 1-877-542-2596.

Library of Congress Cataloging-in-Publication Data

Names: Nagelhout, Ryan, author.
Title: LeBron James / Ryan Nagelhout.
Description: New York : Gareth Stevens Pub., 2017. | Includes index.
Identifiers: LCCN 2016003380 | ISBN 9781482449686 (pbk.) | ISBN 9781482446401 (library bound) | ISBN 9781482446319 (6 pack)
Subjects: LCSH: James, LeBron–Juvenile literature. | Basketball
    players–United States–Biography–Juvenile literature. | African American
    basketball players–United States–Biography–Juvenile literature.
Classification: LCC GV884.J36 N34 2017 | DDC 796.323092–dc23
LC record available at http://lccn.loc.gov/2016003380

Published in 2017 by
Gareth Stevens Publishing
111 East 14th Street, Suite 349
New York, NY 10003

Copyright © 2017 Gareth Stevens Publishing

Designer: Samantha DeMartin
Editor: Ryan Nagelhout

Photo credits: Cover, p. 1 Jason Miller/Getty Images Sport/Getty Images;
p. 5 Steve Grayson/WireImage/Getty Images; p. 7 Al Tielemans/Sports Illustrated/
Getty Images; p. 9 Corey Sipkin/New York Daily News Archive/Getty Images;
p. 11 John Biever/Sports Illustrated/Getty Images; pp. 13, 19 Mike Ehrmann/
Getty Images Sport/Getty Images; p. 15 John W. McDonough/Sports Illustrated/
Getty Images; pp. 17, 21 (Olympics) Christian Petersen/Getty Images Sport/
Getty Images; p. 21 (NBA MVP) Alexander Tamargo/WireImage/Getty Images;
p. 21 (trophies) Incomible/Shutterstock.com.

Printed in the United States of America

CPSIA compliance information: Batch #CS16GS: For further information contact Gareth Stevens, New York, New York at 1-800-542-2595.

CONTENTS

Growing Up LeBron 4

Mr. Basketball 6

Going Pro 8

First Finals 10

The Decision 12

Finally Champion 14

Olympic Star 16

Family Life 18

Return to Cleveland 20

Glossary 22

For More Information 23

Index 24

Boldface words appear in the glossary.

Growing Up LeBron

LeBron James is an NBA superstar. He was born on December 30, 1984, in Akron, Ohio. James grew up poor. He loved basketball and started playing in elementary school. People in Ohio called him a basketball **prodigy**.

Mr. Basketball

James played basketball at St. Vincent–St. Mary High School in Akron. He was named Ohio's Mr. Basketball three times. His team also won the state **championship** three times. James even made the cover of *Sports Illustrated* his junior year!

Going Pro

James went straight to the pros after high school. The forward was picked first overall by the Cleveland Cavaliers in the 2003 NBA **Draft**. Cleveland is about 40 miles (64 km) north of Akron. He got to play for his hometown team!

First Finals

James won the 2004 **Rookie** of the Year **award**. In 2007, he led Cleveland to its first NBA Finals. They lost to the San Antonio Spurs. James won his first NBA Most Valuable Player (MVP) award in 2009.

The Decision

In 2010, James made a big decision. He left Cleveland to play for the Miami Heat. Along with Dwyane Wade and Chris Bosh, he took the Heat to the NBA Finals in 2011. But they lost to the Dallas Mavericks.

Finally Champion

James and the Heat went back to the Finals in 2012. This time, they beat the Oklahoma City Thunder. James won his first NBA title. He was also named Finals MVP. The Heat won the NBA title again in 2013. James was named Finals MVP again!

Olympic Star

James has many **international** awards, too. He led Team USA to two Olympic gold medals. His first was at the 2008 Beijing Olympic Games. The second was in London in 2012. He also won bronze at the 2004 Athens Games.

Family Life

James married his wife, Savannah, in 2013. The two met in high school! They have two sons named LeBron Jr. and Bryce Maximus and a daughter, Zhuri Nova. LeBron Jr., or "Bronny," plays basketball just like his dad!

Return to Cleveland

In 2014, James decided to leave the Heat. He signed back with the Cavaliers as a **free agent**. James and the Cavs went back to the Finals in 2015. James says he wants to win it all with his hometown team!

TROPHY CASE

NBA Rookie of the Year
2003–2004

NBA Title & NBA Finals MVP
2012 2013

NBA MVP
2008–09
2009–10
2011–12
2012–13

Olympic Gold Medal 2008 2012
Olympic Bronze Medal 2004

NBA Rookie of the Year
2003–2004

NBA All-Star Game MVP
2006 2008

GLOSSARY

award: a prize given to someone

championship: the contest to decide the overall winner

draft: to pick players for a team. Also, the act of picking players for a team.

free agent: an athlete able to sign with any team

international: involving two or more countries

prodigy: an unusually talented child

rookie: a first-year player in a professional sport

FOR MORE INFORMATION

BOOKS

Donnelly, Patrick. *The Best NBA Forwards of All Time.* Minneapolis, MN: ABDO Publishing, 2014.

Lohre, Mike. *Six Degrees of LeBron James: Connecting Basketball Stars.* North Mankato, MN: Capstone Press, 2015.

Taylor, Charlotte, and Stephen Feinstein. *LeBron James: Basketball Champion.* New York, NY: Enslow Publishing, 2016.

WEBSITES

LeBron James
nba.com/playerfile/lebron_james
Find more stats and other facts about James here.

The Official Website of LeBron James
lebronjames.com
Find out more about James and what he does with his time on his website.

INDEX

Akron, Ohio 4, 6

Cleveland 8, 10, 12

Cleveland Cavaliers
  8, 20

family 18

Miami Heat 12,
  14, 20

Mr. Basketball 6

MVP 10, 14

NBA Finals 10, 12,
  14, 20

NBA title 14

Olympics 16

Rookie of the Year 10

state championship 6

St. Vincent–St. Mary
  High School 6

Team USA 16